Imagine

Rachel Wilson

Daniel Barber

COURSE CONSULTANTS

Paul Dummett

Elaine Boyd

NATIONAL GEOGRAPHIC
LEARNING

Australia • Brazil • Canada • Mexico • Singapore • United Kingdom • United States

Scope and Sequence

Welcome p. 4

Free Time	fly a kite, make a cake, paint a picture, play a game, play soccer, read a book, sing a song, write a story
Numbers	20 to 100

	Vocabulary	Grammar	Reading	Phonics	Song and Value
1 Animals p. 7 *School Subject: Science*	crocodile, elephant, giraffe, hippo, lion, monkey, snake, tiger, zebra *Reading:* mud, sleep, work, young	Present progressive: *Yes / No* questions Comparatives with *-er*	"A Baby Elephant" Read about a baby elephant.	**a_e** as in: cake game snake	Sing about monkeys. *Value:* Be interested in animals.
2 How's the Weather? p. 15 *School Subject: Science*	cloudy, cold, hot, raining, snowing, sunny, windy, bring an umbrella, put on a scarf, wear a coat *Reading:* brighter, forget, rainbow, sky	*What's* + noun + *like?* and answers using *It's …* Imperatives	"Rainbows" Read about rainbows.	**i_e** as in: bike kite time	Sing about the weather. *Value:* Take care of yourself.
UNITS 1–2	Let's Talk p. 23 Being Polite		Video pp. 24–25 "The National Zoo"		Review p. 26 Units 1–2
3 Let's Go! p. 27 *School Subject: Technology & Engineering*	bus, car, helicopter, motorcycle, plane, ship, truck; come home, get to school, ride a bike *Reading:* healthy, months, ready, snack	Present simple: *Wh-* questions with *How, When,* and *Where* Irregular plurals	"How Bananas Get into Our Hands" Read about knowing our food.	**o_e** as in: home nose cone	Sing about flying in a plane. *Value:* Be safe.
4 Growing Up p. 35 *School Subject: Health & Physical Education*	clean, dirty, kind, little, loud, naughty, quiet, scary, silly, smart *Reading:* cartoons, famous, funny, grown-up	Past simple: *was* Past simple: *were*	"Find Your Talent" Read about Charles Schulz.	**u_e** as in: cube cute tube	Sing about frogs. *Value:* Be curious.
UNITS 3–4	Game p. 43 Spinner Wheel		Reading Challenge pp. 44–45 "Cars: Then and Now"		Review p. 46 Units 3–4

2

Welcome

A Listen and point. 🎧 TR: 0.1

fly a kite

make a cake

paint a picture

play a game

play soccer

read a book

sing a song

write a story

B Listen and repeat. 🎧 TR: 0.2

C Point and say.

Fly a kite!

Make a cake!

4

Lesson 2

A **Listen and read.** 🎧 TR: 0.3

> **Let's fly** a kite!
> **Great idea!**
>
> **Let's play** soccer!
> **No!**

B **Listen and chant.** 🎧 TR: 0.4

Let's make a cake!
Great idea!

Let's fly a kite!
Great idea!

Let's paint a picture of a house!
No! No! A picture of a mouse!

Let's read a book!
Great idea!

Let's play a game!
Great idea!

Let's write a story about a dog!
No! No! A story about a frog!

C **Say.**

Let's sing a song!

No!

OK. Let's paint a picture!

Great idea!

Women painting near
Jodhpur, India

Welcome

A Listen and point. 🎧 TR: 0.5

twenty   thirty   forty   fifty   sixty

seventy   eighty   ninety   one hundred

twenty-one   twenty-two   twenty-three

twenty-four   twenty-five   twenty-six

twenty-seven   twenty-eight   twenty-nine

B Listen and repeat. 🎧 TR: 0.6

C Point and say.   sixty   thirty

1 Animals

A saltwater crocodile, Australia

A **Look and circle.**

1. How many animals do you see?

   1   2   3

2. What do you see?

   sky   trees   water

B **Draw and color something this animal eats.**

Lesson 1 Vocabulary

A Listen and point. 🎧 TR: 1.1

 crocodile

 elephant

 giraffe

 hippo

lion

 monkey

 snake

 tiger

zebra

B Listen and repeat. 🎧 TR: 1.2

C Say.

Can a snake swim?

Yes it can.

A **Listen and read.** 🎧 TR: 1.3

Is the giraffe eat**ing**?	Yes, it **is**.
Are the zebras drink**ing**?	No, they **aren't**.
Are you look**ing** at that giraffe?	Yes, I **am**.
Are you tak**ing** photos?	No, we **aren't**.

B **Listen and chant.** 🎧 TR: 1.4

Oh! There's a tiger. Is the tiger sleeping?
Shh, shh. Yes, it is.

Oh! There's a snake. Is the snake sleeping?
Shh, shh. Yes, it is.

Oh! There's a crocodile. Is the croc sleeping?
Snap, snap! No, it isn't!

Help! There's a crocodile. Is the croc running?
Snap, snap! Yes, it is! SNAP!

C **Look at the photo.** Say.

Is the elephant drinking?

No, it isn't.

Are the zebras sleeping?

No, they aren't.

A giraffe running, Kenya

A Listen and repeat. 🎧 TR: 1.5

> young   work   sleep   mud

B Listen and read. 🎧 TR: 1.6

Naleku is a baby African elephant. She lives at a home for **young** elephants in Kenya, Africa. She doesn't have a mother. The people **work** at the animal home to take care of her. Every day, they give Naleku milk and a lot of love. They **sleep** with her at night, too!

In the day, Naleku goes for a walk with other elephants. They are her friends. Some of the elephants are older than Naleku. They are bigger than Naleku, too.

All of the elephants love water. They like to play in the **mud**. The elephants are very happy. It's fun to watch them!

C Read and circle.

1. Naleku is a **young** / **old** African elephant.

2. The people give Naleku **milk** / **water** every day.

3. **At night** / **In the day**, Naleku goes for a walk with her friends.

4. **Some** / **All** of the elephants love water.

5. They like to **sleep** / **play** in the mud.

A **Listen and read.** 🎧 TR: 1.7

Naleku is **younger than** the other elephants.
The other elephants are **bigger than** Naleku.

B **Listen and check.** 🎧 TR: 1.8

1.

2.

3.

4.

C **Ask and answer.**

Is a hippo bigger than a zebra?

Yes, it is.

Is a tiger slower than a monkey?

No, it isn't.

Naleku in Kenya

A Listen, point, and repeat. 🎧 TR: 1.9

a_e

c**a**ke

g**a**me

snake

B Listen and chant. Circle the words with **a_e**. 🎧 TR: 1.10

Let's play a game of
Snakes and Ladders.
Let's make a cake
and drink lemonade.

Let's get our skateboards
and take them to the park.
Let's go to the lake
and sit in the shade.

A boy skateboarding, India

C Listen. Check the box when you hear **a_e**. 🎧 TR: 1.11

1. ☐   2. ☐   3. ☐   4. ☐   5. ☐   6. ☐

D Listen and write the missing letters with **a_e**. 🎧 TR: 1.12

g_____

pl_____

bookc_____

sk_____

w_____

sn_____

c_____

b_____ball

E Play the *I Spy* game.

cake   chase   grapes   lemonade   plane   wave

A Listen, read, and write. 🎧 TR: 1.13

Some monkeys are climbing up a tree,
and their babies are playing happily.
Are the babies _____? Yes, they are.
They're jumping from tree to tree.
Are they small? Yes, they are.
They're smaller than you and me!

The _____ are getting food in the tree,
and their babies are watching hungrily.
Are the babies _____? Yes, they are.
They're eating fruit from the tree.
Are they hungry? Yes, they are.
They're hungrier than you and me!

Now the monkeys are sitting under the tree,
and holding their babies quietly.
Are the babies sleeping? Yes, they are.
They're _____ in the shade of the tree.
Are they cute? Yes, they are!
But are they _____ than you and me?

Monkeys playing,
Qinling Mountains,
China

B Listen and sing. 🎧 TR: 1.14 and 1.15

C Sing and act. 🎧 TR: 1.16

2 How's the Weather?

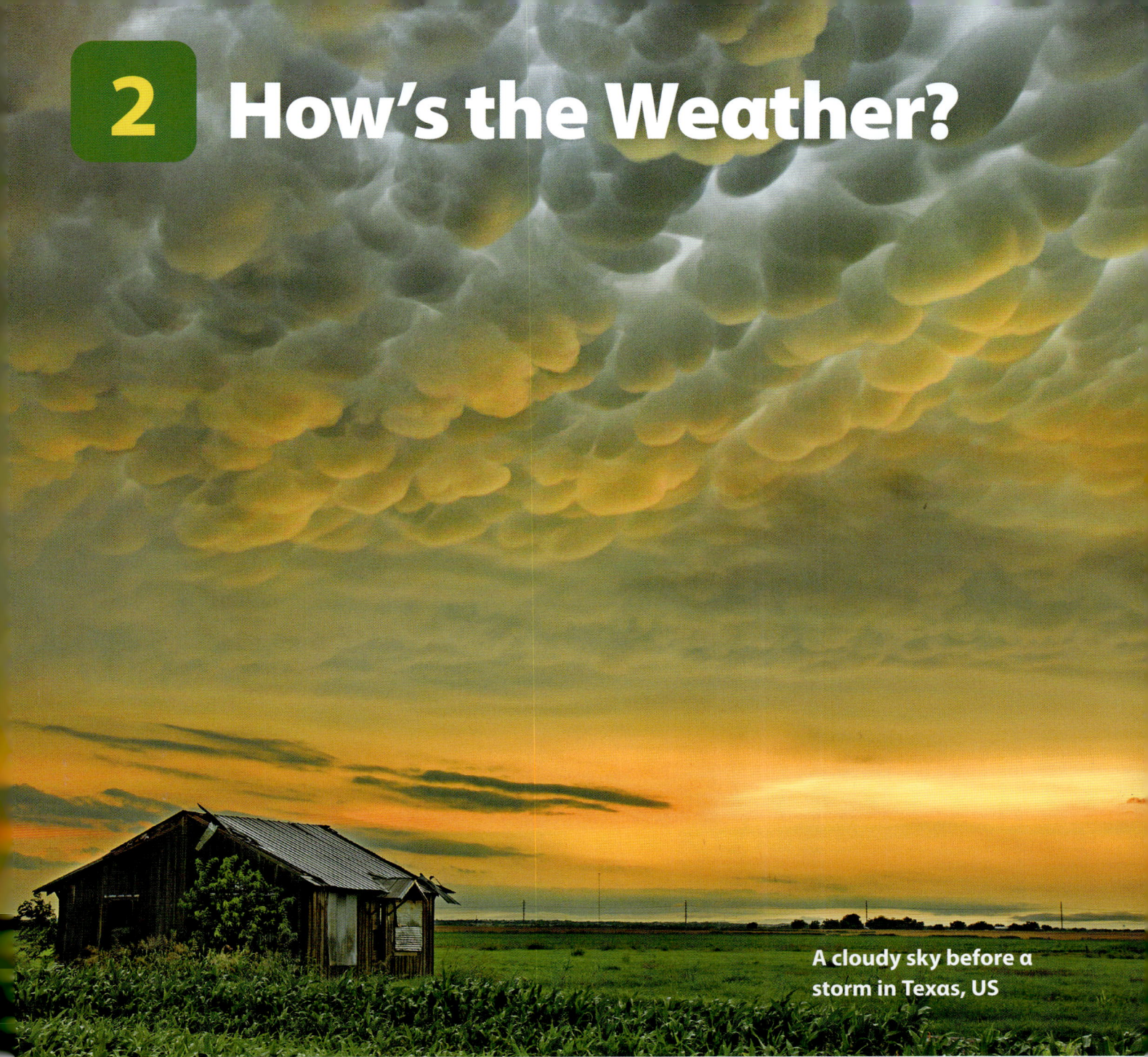

A cloudy sky before a storm in Texas, US

A Look and check the things you see.

- [ ] clouds
- [ ] flowers
- [ ] house
- [ ] sky
- [ ] snake
- [ ] water

B Draw and color the weather today.

A **Listen and point.** 🎧 TR: 2.1

cloudy

cold

hot

raining

snowing

sunny

windy

bring an
umbrella

put on
a scarf

wear a
coat

B **Listen and repeat.** 🎧 TR: 2.2

C **Say.**

Is it windy today?

Yes it is.

Let's fly a kite.

Girls sheltering from the rain, Mirissa, Sri Lanka

A **Listen and read.** 🎧 TR: 2.3

> **What's the weather like?** | It's sunny.
> It's snowing.

B **Listen and chant.** 🎧 TR: 2.4

Hey, hey, what's the weather like?
What's the weather like today?
It's cloudy. It's raining.
I'm wearing my T-shirt.
The weather is hot today!

Hey, hey, what's the weather like?
What's the weather like today?
It's windy. It's snowing.
I'm wearing my coat.
The weather is cold today!

C **Match and say.**

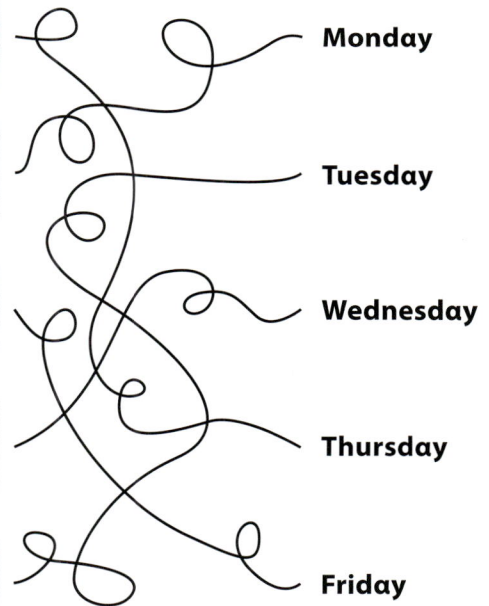

Monday
Tuesday
Wednesday
Thursday
Friday

> What's the weather like on Tuesday?

> It's windy.

UNIT 2   **17**

A Listen and repeat. 🎧 TR: 2.5

sky   rainbow   brighter   forget

B Listen and read. 🎧 TR: 2.6

What is a Rainbow?

It's a colorful arc in the **sky**. A **rainbow** usually has red, orange, yellow, green, blue, and violet. But rainbows don't always have six colors. Morning rainbows are red, orange, and yellow—you can't see the other colors.

What Weather Makes a Rainbow?

Rain and sun make a rainbow. Bigger raindrops make **brighter** rainbows. To find a rainbow, stand with the sun behind you. Don't **forget** your umbrella! Now, look up.

Can I Make a Rainbow?

Yes, you can. Bring a glass of water and some white paper to a sunny window. Hold the glass above the paper. Sunlight goes through the water and makes a rainbow on the paper.

C Read again. Write the correct word.

behind   brighter   violet   water

1. In the morning, you can't see _____ in a rainbow.

2. Rainbows are _____ when the raindrops are bigger.

3. The sun is _____ you when you see a rainbow.

4. Sunlight and _____ make rainbows.

A **Listen and read.** 🎧 TR: 2.7

> **Bring** a glass of water.
> **Don't forget** your umbrella.

B **Listen and circle.** 🎧 TR: 2.8

1. **Wear** / **Don't wear** your boots.

   Don't bring / **Don't forget** your umbrella.

2. **Wear** / **Don't wear** your jeans.

   Put on / **Don't put on** your shorts.

3. **Wear** / **Don't wear** your shoes inside.

   Put / **Don't put** them next to the door.

C **Say the opposite.**

Please put on your scarf.

Don't put on your scarf.

Please wear your gloves.

Don't wear your gloves.

Don't bring your hat.

Please bring your hat.

A rainbow over the
Magdalen Islands, Canada

A **Listen, point, and repeat.** 🎧 TR: 2.9

i_e

b**i**k**e**

k**i**t**e**

t**i**m**e**

B **Listen and chant.** Circle the words with **i_e**. 🎧 TR: 2.10

My name is Mike.   I fly my kite.
I play outside.   I swim and dive.
I ride my bike.   I don't play inside.
That's what I like.   That's not what I like.

C **Listen.** Check the box when you hear **i_e**. 🎧 TR: 2.11

1. ☐   2. ☐   3. ☐   4. ☐   5. ☐   6. ☐

D **Listen and write the missing letters with i_e.** 🎧 TR: 2.12

1.

b_____

3.

f_____

5.

d_____

7.

l_____

2.

t_____

4.

outs_____

6.

sm_____

8.

crocod_____

E **Listen and write the letters.** Then play the game and say the words. 🎧 TR: 2.13

Start

= 1 space

= 2 spaces

End

f_____

d_____

b_____

sm_____

h_____

l_____

t_____

k_____

n_____

pr_____

A **Listen, read, and write.** 🎧 TR: 2.14

CHORUS

What's the weather like?
It's snowing today!
It's _____ and gray,
but that's OK!

It's seven o'clock and we get up.
We look outside and…it's _____!
Quick! Put on your coat.
Put on your _____ and gloves.
Put on your _____. Don't forget that!
Let's go outside and play in the snow.

CHORUS

It's twelve o'clock and we're feeling cold.
We look inside and…we're hungry!
Quick! Take off your _____.
Take off your scarf and gloves.
Take off your hat. Don't forget that!
Let's go inside and eat our lunch.

B **Listen and sing.** 🎧 TR: 2.15 and 2.16

C **Sing and act.** 🎧 TR: 2.17

A girl plays in the snow, Puerto Williams, Chile

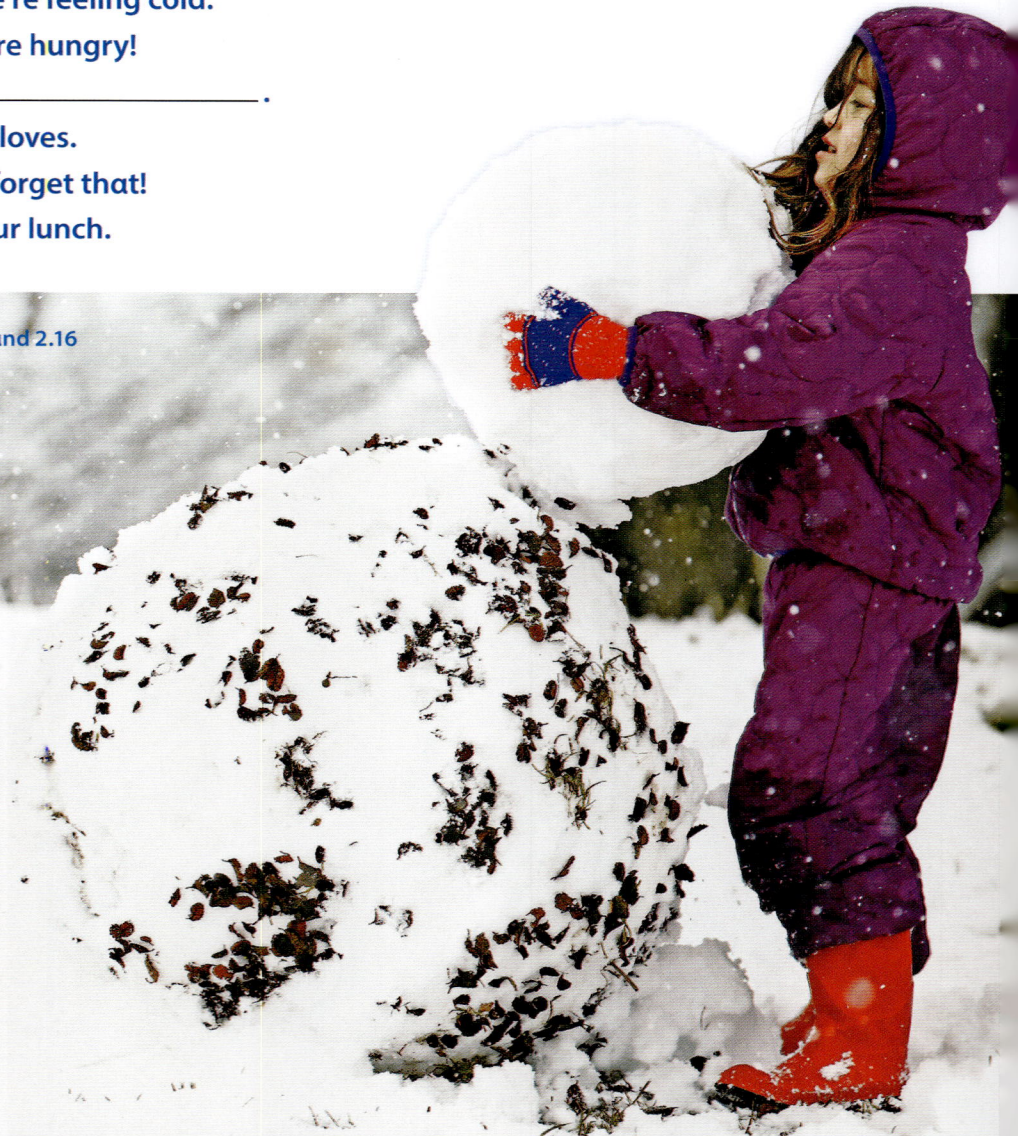

Excuse me.   Sure. Here you are.
Can I please see/have…?   I'm sorry. I don't have…
I'd like…   That's OK.

A **Listen and write.** 🎧 TR: 2.18

Lea: Excuse _____ 1. . Can I please see that red hat?

Store clerk: Sure. Here _____ 2. .

Lea: Oh, it's too small. Can I _____ 3. have a bigger one?

Store clerk: I'm _____ 4. . I don't have a bigger hat in red.

Lea: That's _____ 5. . Oh, I love that blue hat. Can I see it?

Store clerk: _____ 6. . Here you are. It looks great on you!

Lea: Thanks! _____ 7. this hat. How much is it?

Store clerk: It's ten euros.

Lea: _____ 8. you are: ten euros.

Store clerk: Thank you! Have a nice day!

B **Listen, check, and repeat.** 🎧 TR: 2.19

C **Read.** Circle the more polite choice.

1. **a** Hey! Give me that scarf.

   b Excuse me. Can you please give me that scarf?

2. **a** I'd like an umbrella, please.

   b I want an umbrella.

3. **a** Sure. Here you are.

   b Here. Take it.

4. **a** No blue gloves.

   b I'm sorry. I don't have any blue gloves.

D **Say Activity A with a partner.** Act out a similar dialogue. Use your own words.

The National Zoo

Pandas live at the National Zoo in Washington, D.C., in the United States. The zookeepers—people who work at the zoo—take good care of the pandas. They study them, too. This helps people around the world understand pandas better. Today is a very special day at the zoo. It's Tian Tian's birthday! Let's celebrate with him!

A **Look, read, and circle.**

1. This is a photo of a **bear** / **zebra**.

2. It's in a **park** / **zoo**.

3. It's **walking** / **drinking**.

B **What's in Tian Tian's cake?** Circle the ingredients. ▶ Video 1

bamboo	pears
beans	potatoes
carrots	rice
eggs	water

C **Answer the questions in pairs.**

1. How old is Tian Tian?

2. What do pandas eat every day?

3. What shape is Tian Tian's birthday cake?

4. What does Tian Tian do with his cake?

5. Do you like Tian Tian's cake? Do you want to eat it? Why or why not?

D **PROJECT** **You want to make something for a special day.** Who's it for? What do you make? How do you make it? Draw and write.

E **Present your drawing to the class.**

For Mother's Day, I make Mom her favorite banana cake. I use eggs, bananas, oil…

Bolo de banana

Tian Tian at the National Zoo in Washington, D.C., US

A **Look.** Unscramble and write.

1.
nunys

____ ____ ____ ____ ____

2.
ninarig

____ ____ ____ ____ ____ ____ ____

3.
dwniy

____ ____ ____ ____ ____

4.
yducol

____ ____ ____ ____ ____ ____

B **Listen and circle.** 🎧 TR: 2.20

1. It's **raining / sunny**. **Put on / Don't wear** your boots.

2. It's **hot / cloudy**. **Don't bring / Don't forget** your sun hat.

3. It's **windy / raining**. **Wear / Don't wear** your scarf.

4. It's **sunny / cloudy**. **Bring / Don't bring** your coat.

C **Look and read.** Write *Yes* or *No*.

1. The zebra is drinking water.

_____

2. It's raining.

_____

3. The hippo is bigger than the rhino.

_____

4. The baby elephant is taking a bath.

_____

5. The snake is longer than the crocodile.

_____

3 # Let's Go!

A monorail in Seattle, US

A **Look and circle.**

1. How many people are there?

   2   3   4

2. What color do you see?

   green   pink   purple

B **Draw and color a way you travel.**

A Listen and point. 🎧 TR: 3.1

bus

car

helicopter

motorcycle

plane

ship

truck

come home

get to school

ride a bike

B Listen and repeat. 🎧 TR: 3.2

C Say.

Are you riding a bike?

Yes, I am.

Girls ride bikes home
from school, Laos

A Listen and read. 🎧 TR: 3.3

> **How do** you **get to** school?
> I go by bus.
>
> **When does** the bus **come**?
> It comes at 7:00.
>
> **Where does** the bus **go**?
> It goes to the library.

B Listen and chant. 🎧 TR: 3.4

How do you get to school?
By bus, or car, or train?
I go to school by bus.
Then it brings me home again.

When does your school bus come?
At six, or seven, or eight?
It comes at seven o'clock,
but now and then it's late!

Where does your school bus go
after you get to school?
It goes past the library, the stores,
the playground, and the pool.

C Say.

How do you get to school?

I go by train.

When do you go?

I go at 8:00.

A Listen and repeat. 🎧 TR: 3.5

healthy   snack   months   ready

B Listen and read. 🎧 TR: 3.6

Bananas are a **healthy snack**. They grow in hot, sunny countries. So, how do bananas get into stores around the world?

1 Bananas start as flowers on a banana plant. After about nine **months**, the farmer takes the bunch off the plant. They're still green.

2 Workers look at the bananas. If the bananas look OK, the workers put them into boxes. These boxes of bananas go by truck to a shipyard.

3 Now the bananas are **ready** for a long trip. They go by ship to different countries. It can take more than fourteen days.

4 Then trucks bring the bananas to towns and cities. There, workers in stores put the bananas out. Now people can buy the bananas. When they're yellow, they're ready to eat!

C Put the sentences in order.

The bananas start as flowers on a plant. ☐

The bananas are yellow and ready to eat. ☐

The bananas go into boxes. ☐

The bananas go by truck to the stores. ☐

The bananas go by ship to different countries. ☐

Bananas on a ship, Nicaragua

A **Listen and read.** 🎧 TR: 3.7

One	Two or more	One	Two or more
baby	babies	child	children
beach	beaches	fish	fish
box	boxes	foot	feet
bus	buses	man	men
dish	dishes	mouse	mice
scarf	scarves	person	people
tomato	tomatoes	sheep	sheep

B **Look and write.** Listen and check. 🎧 TR: 3.8

1. _____   3. _____   5. _____

2. _____   4. _____   6. _____

C **Find and count these things in your classroom.**

box   child   dress   foot   lunch   scarf   woman

There are ten children.
There aren't any scarves.

A Listen, point, and repeat. 🎧 TR: 3.9

o_e

home

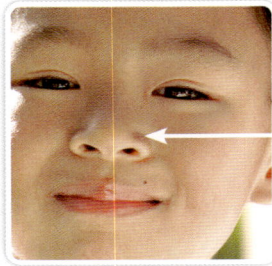
nose

cone

B Listen and chant. Circle the words with **o_e**. 🎧 TR: 3.10

Queen Rose is at home.
She sits all alone
on her beautiful throne,
eating a cone.

What's that on her nose
and her wonderful throne?
Not ice cream, I hope –
on those beautiful clothes!

C **Listen.** Check the box when you hear **o_e**. 🎧 TR: 3.11

1. ☐   2. ☐   3. ☐   4. ☐   5. ☐   6. ☐

D **Listen and write the missing letters with o_e.** 🎧 TR: 3.12

1.
c_____

3.
dr_____

5.
h_____

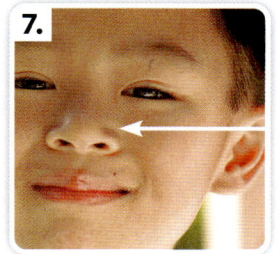
7.
n_____

2.
r_____

4.
b_____

6.
thr_____

8.
n_____book

E **Play.**

notebook

+1   throne

nose   bone

rope   +1

home

drone

cone   +1

rope

globe

END

START

🪙 = 1 space

🪙 = 2 spaces

A **Listen, read, and write.** 🎧 TR: 3.13

CHORUS

I'm going on a trip,
but I'm not going by _____ .
I'm not going by _____ .
I'm getting there by plane!

I'm inside the plane, ready to fly.
I'm sitting by the little window.
I'm feeling _____ . It's my first time in the sky.
Seat belts on and up we go!

CHORUS

Up and through the clouds, we're flying high.
Outside the sky's a beautiful blue.
I look down at the towns and the cities below.
Tiny _____ , buses, and trucks, too!

CHORUS

I eat some _____ and I watch TV.
Outside my window, I can see snow!
I'm really far from home, but that's just fine by me.
Seat belts on and down we go!

B **Listen and sing.** 🎧 TR: 3.14 and 3.15

C **Sing and act.** 🎧 TR: 3.16

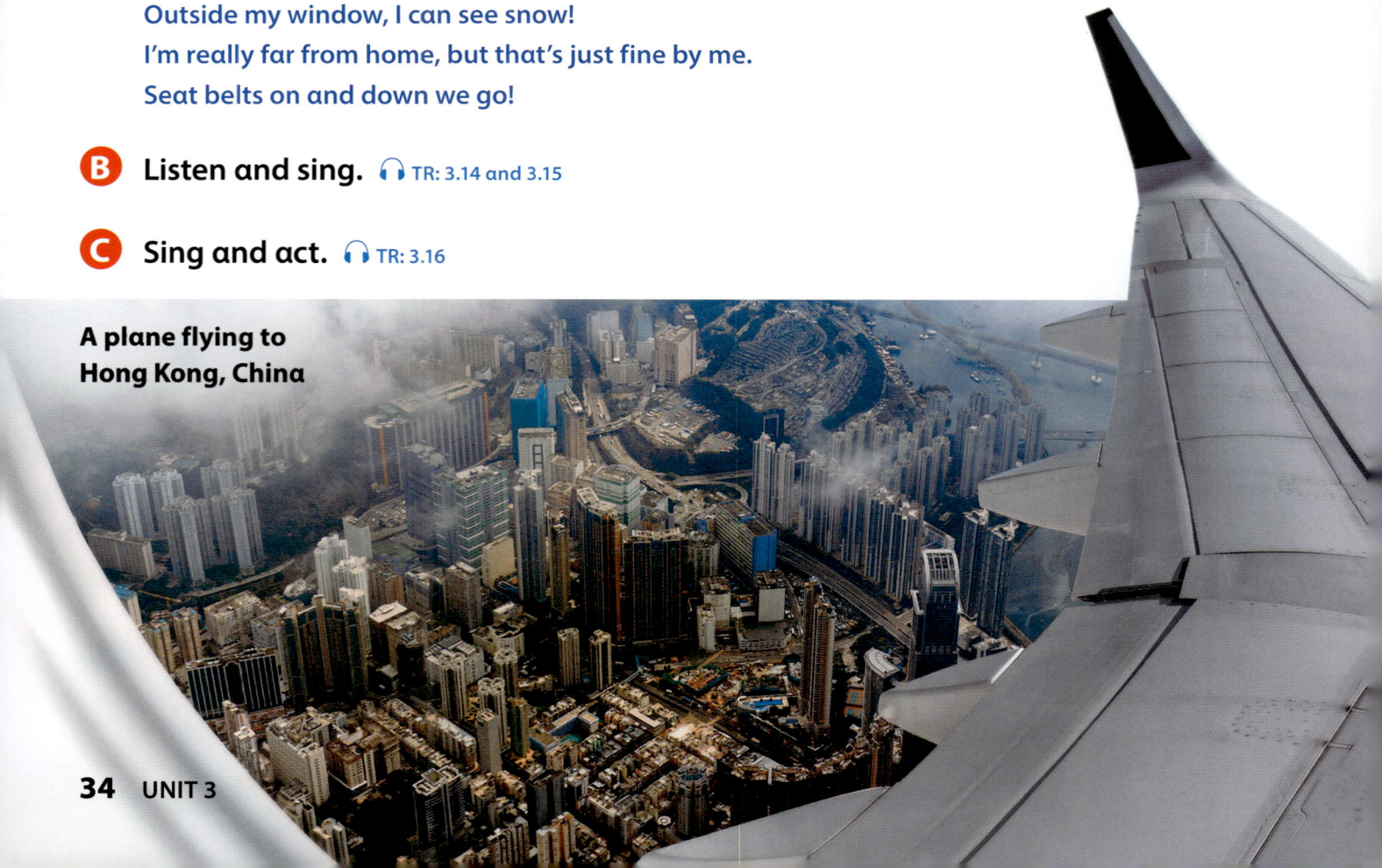

A plane flying to Hong Kong, China

4 Growing Up

A mother bear and cubs
near Kurile Lake, Russia

A Look and circle.

1. How many baby bears do you see?

   2   3   4

2. What are the bears doing?

   drinking   eating   playing

B Draw and color you when you were a baby.

A Listen and point. 🎧 TR: 4.1

clean

dirty

kind

little

loud

naughty

quiet

scary

silly

smart

B Listen and repeat. 🎧 TR: 4.2

C Say.

You're loud!

Yes, I am!

A boy playing with his shadow

A **Listen and read.** 🎧 TR: 4.3

> When I was little,...
> I **was** good.
> I **wasn't** naughty.
>
> This story **was** scary.
> It **wasn't** silly.

B **Listen and chant.** 🎧 TR: 4.4

Growing up, growing up!
I was loud at three years old.
I was naughty at four years old.
I was kind at five years old.

Growing up, growing up!
I was quiet at six years old.
I was silly at seven years old.
Now I'm eight, I'm as good as gold!

C **Say.**

> What were you like when you were little?

> When I was little, I was silly.

> That's funny.
> Now you are smart!
> When I was little, I was loud.

> Me too! I wasn't quiet when I was little.

A **Listen and repeat.** 🎧 TR: 4.5

funny   cartoons   grown-up   famous

B **Listen and read.** 🎧 TR: 4.6

Charles was a quiet boy. He wasn't good at schoolwork or sports. Some of his classmates weren't very kind to him. But Charles was good at art. His pictures were very **funny**. They were fantastic!

Look at the photo. Do you know this dog? It's Snoopy. Charles is Charles Schulz, the creator of Snoopy and the *Peanuts* **cartoons**. Today, people around the world love this silly black-and-white dog, his owner Charlie Brown, and their friends, the *Peanuts* gang.

As a child, Charles Schulz's life wasn't easy. As a **grown-up**, Charles Schulz was a **famous** artist. Art was his talent. What's your talent?

C **Answer the questions.**

1. What was Charles like as a child?
2. What was Charles good at?
3. What was Charles as a grown-up?
4. What's your talent?

Charles Schulz with a *Peanuts* cartoon

A **Listen and read.** 🎧 TR: 4.7

> Some of the students **were** naughty.
> They **weren't** kind.
>
> In art class, we **were** dirty!
> We **weren't** clean.
>
> You **were** good at art.
> You **weren't** good at sports.

B **Listen and complete.** Check the sentences in the past. 🎧 TR: 4.8

1. _____ not famous. ☐

2. The children _____ silly at the party. ☐

3. My cousin _____ very smart. ☐

4. We _____ quiet at the library. ☐

5. The story _____ so funny. ☐

C **Look and say.**

	loud	smart	kind
Mike and Kate	✓	✗	✓
Rose and Cole	✗	✓	✓
Lily and James	✓	✓	✗

Mike and Kate were loud when they were little.

Rose and Cole weren't loud when they were little.

Lily and James were loud when they were little.

A **Listen, point, and repeat.** 🎧 TR: 4.9

u_e

cu**b**e

cu**t**e

tu**b**e

B **Listen and chant.** Circle the words with **u_e**. 🎧 TR: 4.10

A cute little boy
is sitting at home.
With a little toy flute,
he plays a tune.

He decides to use
some cubes of ice
in a huge lemonade.
Mmmm, very good!

A boy playing
a flute

C **Listen.** Check the box when you hear **u_e**. 🎧 TR: 4.11

1. ☐   2. ☐   3. ☐   4. ☐   5. ☐   6. ☐

D **Listen and write the missing letters with u_e.** 🎧 TR: 4.12

1.

c_____

3.

d_____

5.

h_____

7.

m_____

2.

t_____

4.

c_____

6.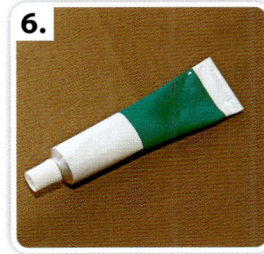

t_____

8.

J_____

E **Listen and write the letters.** Then play the game and say the words. 🎧 TR: 4.13

🪙 = 1 space   🪙 = 2 spaces

start

h_____

c_____   m_____

d_____   c_____   fl_____

J_____

r_____   r_____   m_____   end

A **Listen, read, and write.** 🎧 TR: 4.14

A lot of little tadpoles _____ in the pond.

Their bodies were black and their tails were long.

They weren't loud—they were quiet.

They were _____ and cute!

This is how they were when they were young.

But that was then.

They're different now.

Their bodies change.

Let me tell you how.

Now a lot of _____ frogs are in the pond.

Their bodies are green and their tails are gone.

They aren't quiet—they're _____ !

They're big but not _____ !

Now they can jump around because their legs are strong.

B **Listen and sing.** 🎧 TR: 4.15 and 4.16

C **Sing and act.** 🎧 TR: 4.17

Tadpoles in La Pampa, Argentina

A **Spin.** Look and say.

When I was little, I was loud.

me

weather

big

get to town

get to school

weather

fast

brother/sister/cousin

Player 1

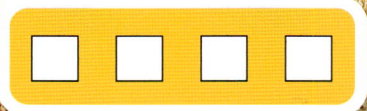

Player 2

Cars: Then and Now

Cars are different now than they were in the past. Let's take a look!

1880s

Karl Benz makes one of the first cars. It has three wheels, and it's faster than a horse or a bicycle. In 1888, his wife Bertha is the first person to go by car on a long trip. The trip is only 105 kilometers, but it takes Bertha about twelve hours!

1910s

Henry Ford and his team make the famous Ford Model T car. Now a lot of people can get a car.

The Model T has four wheels, but it only has one window in the front.

1950s

Cars are every color of the rainbow, including pink! They're bigger and faster than the early cars. These cars make the air dirty, but people aren't thinking much about this. They're just enjoying their big, colorful cars!

Glossary

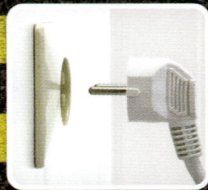

air

electric

wheel

A **Read and guess.**

It has mirrors, doors, and windows, but it's not a house. You can sit down, but it's not a chair. Your body doesn't move, but you go to different places. What is it? _____

B **Listen and read.** About how old are cars? Circle the number of years. 🎧 TR: 4.18

a. 140   b. 100   c. 50

C **Read again.** Match.

1. Some cars are electric. In others, there's no driver.   1880s

2. Cars were big. There were a lot of different colors, like pink!   1910s

                                                              1950s

3. There was only one window.   Today

4. There were only three wheels.

Today

Today's cars are smaller than cars in the 1950s. Some cars are electric. People like electric cars because the air stays cleaner. They're also quieter than normal cars. Scientists are even making cars with no drivers. That's amazing!

D **Compare cars and bikes.** Write.

cars	fast
bikes	slow

E **Talk about Activity D in pairs.**

Cars are faster than bikes.

Yes, but bikes are quieter than cars.

A Look and read. Write (✓) or (✗) in the box.

1. ☐ This is a helicopter.

2. ☐ These are motorcycles.

3. ☐ This is a ship.

4. ☐ These are trucks.

B Write.

1. a box ⟶ some boxes

2. a bus ⟶ some _____

3. a child ⟶ some _____

4. a man ⟶ some _____

5. a beach ⟶ some _____

6. a mango ⟶ some _____

C Listen and check. 🎧 TR: 4.19

1. How do they get to school?

a   b   c

2. What time do they go to school?

a   b   c

3. How does Dad get to work?

a   b   c

D Read and write.

1. When I was a baby, I _____.

2. When my mom was little, she _____.

3. When my friends and I were little, we _____.

4. When my grandparents were younger, they _____.

5 Our Amazing World

A girl outside of
Yekaterinburg Arena
Stadium during the
FIFA World Cup, Russia

A **Look and circle.**

1. The girl is *laughing* / *singing*.

2. She is *excited* / *scared*.

3. She might be going home *by plane* /
by motorcycle.

B **Work in pairs.** Discuss.

1. Do you like to travel? Why?

2. Where do you want to visit? Why?

A Listen and point. 🎧 TR: 5.1

B Listen and repeat. 🎧 TR: 5.2

North America

the US

the UK

Poland

Europe

Spain

Italy

Africa

South America

Brazil

Argentina

South Africa

C Ask and answer.

What's this country?

It's Brazil.

Correct!

Antarctica

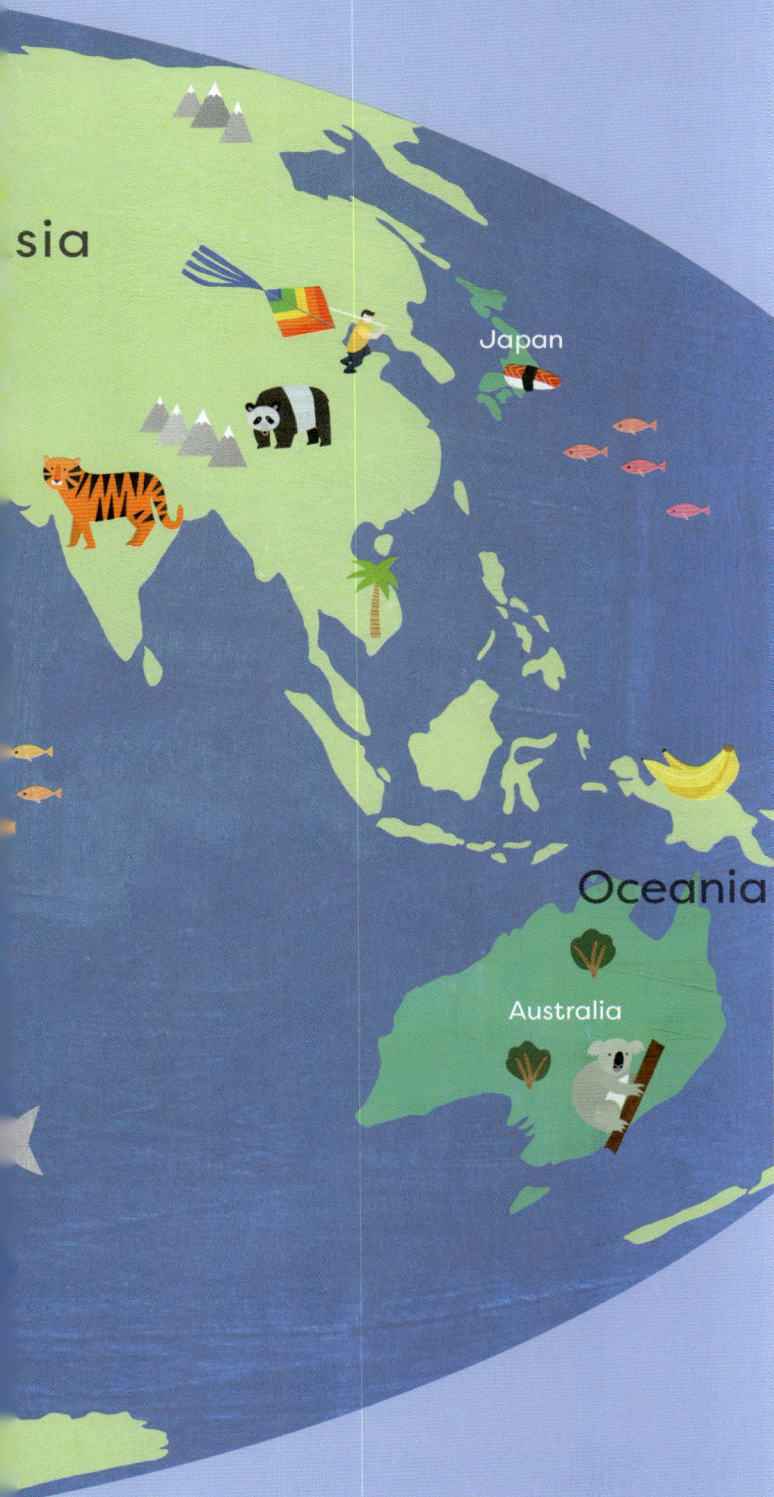

A **Listen and read.** 🎧 TR: 5.3

> **Are** you **from** Japan?
> Yes, **I am.**
>
> Where **are** you **from**?
> **I'm from** Japan.
>
> Where **is** she **from**?
> **She's from** Brazil.

B **Listen and chant.** 🎧 TR: 5.4

Hello! Ciao! Konnichiwa!

Sawubona! Cześć! Hey! Hola!

Where are you from? Are you from Japan?

Yes, yes, I am. I'm from Japan.

And where is he from?

He's from the US.

And where is she from?

She's from Brazil.

So many countries—so many friends.

Let's travel the world. The fun never ends.

C **Play.**

Hi. What's your name?

My name's Sophie.

Are you from Argentina?

No, I'm not.

Are you from Spain?

Yes, I am.

sia

Japan

Oceania

Australia

A **Listen and repeat.** 🎧 TR: 5.5

> hippos   son   daughter   parents

B **Listen and read.** 🎧 TR: 5.6

> Tonie and Shirley Joubert live in South Africa. Their farm is next to a river. They don't have children; they have two **hippos** named Richie and Jessica. The hippos are like their **son** and **daughter**. They think that the Jouberts are their **parents**.
>
> Every day, Jessica and Richie swim in the river. Richie is younger than Jessica. They spend time with other hippos. They also like to spend time with the Jouberts! They come to the house every day. Shirley gives them lots of vegetables. Jessica likes to drink bottles of warm tea. She goes into the house, too.
>
> Visitors can go to the farm every day. You can give Jessica a snack and some tea!

C **Read again.** Write *T* (true) or *F* (false).

1. The Jouberts live next to the ocean. ☐
2. They have three children. ☐
3. Jessica is older than Richie. ☐
4. The Jouberts spend time with other hippos. ☐
5. Richie and Jessica eat vegetables. ☐
6. You can't visit the farm on Sundays. ☐

A Listen and read. 🎧 TR: 5.7

> Hippos are **my** favorite animal.
> **Your** job is to give Jessica a snack.
> **His** grandparents are in Australia.
> **Her** favorite drink is warm tea.
> **Our** school is in South Africa.
> **Their** farm is next to a river.

B Circle the correct answer. Listen and check. 🎧 TR: 5.8

1. Tonie and *his / our / your* wife live in South Africa.
2. *Her / His / Their* name is Shirley.
3. *My / Their / Your* home is near a river.
4. Shirley: "*His / My / Your* job is to give the hippos vegetables."
5. Tonie and Shirley: "*Her / His / Our* hippos are like children."
6. What about you? What are *her / our / your* favorite animals?

C Say.

> best friend   favorite singer   mother

What's the name of your best friend?

His name is Nick.

What's the name of your favorite singer?

Her name is Taylor Swift.

What's the name of your mother?

Her name is Michiko.

Jessica the hippo on a porch with a dog, South Africa

A **Listen and say.** 🎧 TR: 5.9

a_e

pl**a**n**e**

ai

tr**ai**n

ay

pl**ay**

B **Listen. Say the sounds.** 🎧 TR: 5.10

pl – ane   pl**a**n**e**
g – ame   g**a**m**e**
tr – ai – n   tr**ai**n
p – ai – nt   p**ai**nt
pl – ay   pl**ay**
Fr – i – d – ay   Frid**ay**

C **Write a_e, ai, or ay. Listen and chant.**
🎧 TR: 5.11

It's Frid____!
Do you want to pl____ a g____?
We're in the big school pl____ ground.
Let's m____ a tr____n or p____nt a pl____,
play b____ball on our sk____boards!
Hooray!

D Write *a_e*, *ai*, or *ay*. Say the words. Listen and repeat. 🎧 TR: 5 .12

1.

c_____

2.

cr_____ons

3.

pl_____

4.

r_____n

5.

sn_____

6.
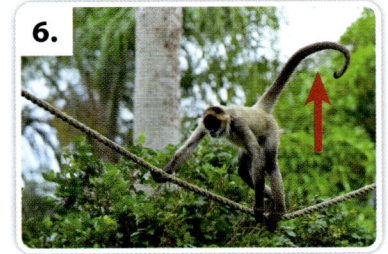
t_____l

E Spin. Say the word.

ai

a_e

ay

say
rain
skateboard
snake
playground
tray
tail
baseball

A **Listen, read, and write.** 🎧 TR: 5.13

Hello, what are you? Do you want to play?
I'm a kind of animal, but I cannot say.
What do you look like?
My ears are big, and I'm big and gray.
Where are you _____?
I'm from South Africa.
Are you an _____?
Yes, I am!

Hello, what are you? Do you want to play?
I'm a sport, but I cannot say.
What are you _____?
I'm fun. I'm fast.
Where are you from?
I'm from the US.
Are you _____?
Yes, I am.

B **Listen and sing.** 🎧 TR: 5.14 and 5.15

C **Sing and act.** 🎧 TR: 5.16

A male elephant, Serengeti
National Park, Tanzania

6 Here and There

A kayaker on a lake,
New Hampshire, US

A Look and circle.

1. The boat is *large / small*.
2. The boat is *in the water / on the land*.
3. It's *raining / sunny*.
4. It's *loud / quiet*.

B Work in pairs. Discuss.

1. How does the photo make you feel?
2. Do you want to do this? Why?

A Listen and point. 🎧 TR: 6.1

farm

field

forest

lake

mountain

path

river

town

village

waterfall

B Listen and repeat. 🎧 TR: 6.2

C Draw and say.

Is it a farm?

No, it isn't.

Is it a field?

Yes. It's a field!

A Listen and read. 🎧 TR: 6.3

> **Do** you **live** in a town?
> Yes, we **do**.
> No, we **don't**.
> No, we **live** in a village.
>
> **Does** Ana **live** next to a forest?
> Yes, she **does**.
> No, she **doesn't**.
> No, she **lives** next to a lake.

B Listen and chant. 🎧 TR: 6.4

Do you live in a town?
Do you live in the countryside?

No, we don't.
Yes, we do.
We live on a farm.

Does she live on a mountain?
Does she live in a forest?

No, she doesn't.
Yes, she does.
She lives in a tree.

Do they live near a river?
Do they live on a lake?

No, they don't.
Yes, they do.
They live on a boat.

C Look and say. Check.

	In a village?	In a town?	Near a river?	Next to a lake?	Near school?
Carlos		✓		✓	✓
Lily	✓		✓		
Rita and Lucas	✓		✓		
You					
Your friend					

Does Carlos live in a village?

No, he doesn't.

Does he live in a town?

Yes, he does!

Right!

Lesson 3 Reading

A **Listen and repeat.** 🎧 TR: 6.5

> subway   on foot   donkey   canoe

B **Listen and read.** 🎧 TR: 6.6

How do you get to school every day? Do you go by bus or by **subway**? Do you go **on foot**? Children get to school in many different ways.

Matheus and his cousins live on a farm in Brazil. Their school is seven kilometers (about four miles) away from the farm. They ride a **donkey** to school every day.

Alicia and her friends don't ride a donkey. They go in a **canoe** across a river to get to school. It's a lot of fun.

Esmeralda and Patricia go to school on foot. They walk along paths, through forests, and even under fences. They walk four hours each day to get to school and back home!

C **Read again.** Write *T* (true) or *F* (false).

1. Matheus and his sisters live on a farm. ☐
2. Matheus walks to school every day. ☐
3. Alicia rides a donkey to school. ☐
4. Esmeralda and Patricia travel far to school. ☐

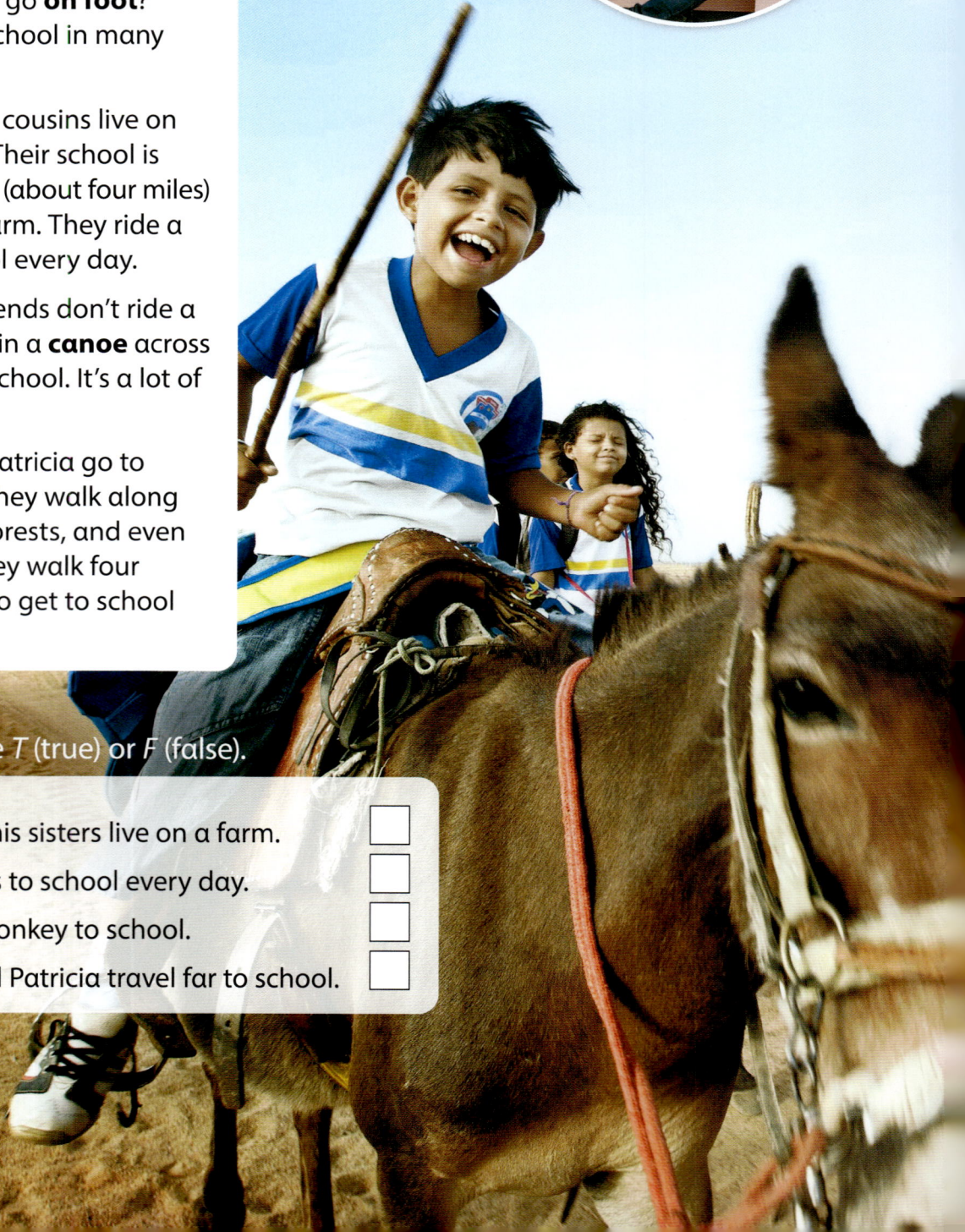

Kids riding donkeys to school, Brazil

A **Listen and read.** 🎧 TR: 6.7

1. They go **across** a river on a canoe.
2. They travel **under** the city on the subway.
3. They ride **above** the city in a helicopter.
4. They walk **through** forests.
5. They walk **down** the mountain.
6. They ride **past** their friends.
7. They go **around** the city on a special bike.
8. They go **along** paths.

B **Listen and circle.** 🎧 TR: 6.8

1.
2.
3.
4.

C **Say two true sentences and one false sentence about your trip to school.** Guess!

I walk to school. I go under a bridge. I don't go past a bookstore.

You don't go under a bridge!

You're right. I don't.

UNIT 6　**59**

A Listen and say. 🎧 TR: 6.9

ee

tr**ee**

ea

b**ea**ch

y

bab**y**

B Listen. Say the sounds. 🎧 TR: 6.10

tr – ee   tr**ee**

b – ea – ch   b**ea**ch

c – ou – n – tr – y countr**y**

w – ee – k   w**ee**k

pl – ea – se   pl**ea**se

st – o – r – y   stor**y**

C Write *ee*, *ea*, or *y*. Listen and chant. 🎧 TR: 6.11

Play on the b_____ch,

climb a tall tr_____,

sail on the s_____,

follow a b_____!

When I go to the countr_____side,

it makes me happ_____ inside!

D Write *ee*, *ea*, or *y*. Say the words. Listen and repeat. 🎧 TR: 6.12

1.

tr_____

2.
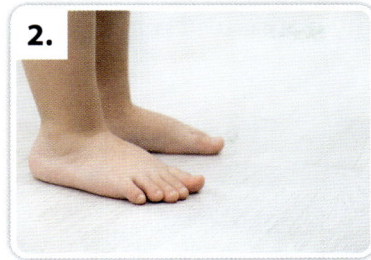
f_____t

3.

j_____ns

4.

bab_____

5.

dirt_____

6.

p_____s

E Follow the words with the same spelling pattern.

A Listen, read, and write. 🎧 TR: 6.13

Do you want to come to my house and play?

Is it far? Can I stay all day?

Sure! There are lots of toys!

For girls and boys?

Yes, let me tell you the _____.

You go down the path, (down the _____)

between the trees, (between the trees)

_____ the beach, (along the beach)

and you're there! (I'm here!)

You go across the _____, (across the river)

past the farm, (past the farm)

under the waterfall, (_____ the waterfall)

and you're there! (I'm here!)

B Listen and sing. 🎧 TR: 6.14 and 6.15

C Sing and act. 🎧 TR: 6.16

Today is **October 1st**. My birthday is on **July 7th**.

Ordinal Numbers 🎧 TR: 6.17

1st	first	7th	seventh	13th	thirteenth
2nd	second	8th	eighth	14th	fourteenth
3rd	third	9th	ninth	20th	twentieth
4th	fourth	10th	tenth	21st	twenty-first
5th	fifth	11th	eleventh	30th	thirtieth
6th	sixth	12th	twelfth		

Months of the Year 🎧 TR: 6.18

January	July
February	August
March	September
April	October
May	November
June	December

A **Listen, read, and write.** 🎧 TR: 6.19

Pablo: What are you doing, Gloria?

Gloria: I'm making party invitations.

Pablo: But today's _____! Your birthday isn't until _____!

Gloria: I know, but they're not for my party. They're invitations for Celina's birthday party.

Pablo: Oh, I see! Well, when's Celina's birthday?

Gloria: Her birthday is on _____. That's Wednesday, and the party's on Sunday, _____. Do you want to come?

Pablo: Yes, I do! Thanks! And you can come to my birthday party on _____.

B **Listen, check, and repeat.** 🎧 TR: 6.20

C **Listen again.** Match. 🎧 TR: 6.21

1. Gloria's birthday   March 16th

2. today   March 18th

3. Celina's birthday   March 22nd

4. Celina's party   April 4th

5. Pablo's party   November 9th

D **Say.**

When's your birthday, Beatriz?

My birthday is on June 30th.

The Sami and the Reindeer

Today we're going to a place where it is very difficult to live—the cold north! Sápmi is a region in the north of Europe. There is snow for a lot of the year, and there are some weeks when you don't see the sun! It isn't easy to travel, play outside, or grow vegetables. But Sápmi is where the Sami people live. It is their home. Let's go and find out how they live.

A **Read and answer.**

1. Where is Sápmi?

2. Why is it difficult to live there?

3. Who lives there?

B **Watch the video.** Circle. ▶ Video 2

1. The reindeer are important to the Sami for **travel** / **food**.

2. The reindeer find food **in the water** / **under the snow**.

3. The reindeer walk far because **the Sami people move them** / **they need to find food**.

4. The Sami reindeer herders live in **one place** / **different places**.

5. The reindeer **swim across the river** / **cross the river in boats**.

C **PROJECT** Draw a map of an imaginary **place.** What animals live there? Choose a place to live on the map.

D **Present your map to the class.**

Many lions, elephants, and zebras live here. I want to live near the elephants...

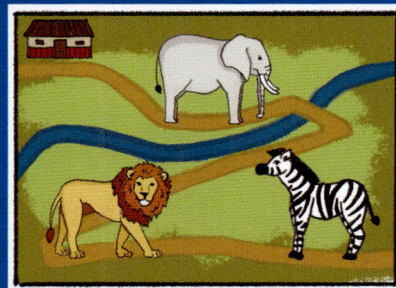

A Sami man and his reindeer

A Write.

1. It _____ _____ _____

2. Br _____ _____ _____ _____

3. Ar _____ _____ _____ _____ _____ _____ _____

4. S _____ _____ _____ h A _____ _____ _____ _____ _____

5. Ja _____ _____ _____

6. Aus _____ _____ _____ _____ _____ _____

B Cross out the incorrect word.

1. Many young people live here, in this **lake / town / village**.

2. You can swim in the **farm / lake / river**.

3. Lots of wild animals live in this **field / forest / village**.

4. Let's walk through this **forest / town / mountain**.

5. That's a very high **river / mountain / waterfall**.

C Write the correct word.

> her   his   my   our   their   your

1. I have a blue bike. I ride _____ bike to school.

2. Victor often walks to school with _____ friends.

3. "Are _____ parents from Argentina?" "No, they're from Spain."

4. There's a new girl in class today. _____ name is Mae.

5. We love monkeys. _____ favorite monkeys live in Brazil.

6. Gina and Raul walk to school. _____ house isn't far.

D Listen and circle the best answer. 🎧 TR: 6.22

1. **a.** No, I don't.

   b. No, he doesn't.

2. **a.** Yes, I am.

   b. It's a big country.

3. **a.** No, he doesn't. He lives in a village.

   b. No, I don't. My house is far away.

4. **a.** Yes, she walks through the park.

   b. No, she can't go to school today.

5. **a.** In a big house near the river.

   b. No, they don't live here.

7 Helping Out

Girls near the beach,
Sri Lanka

A **Look and circle.**

1. The girls are *at the beach* / *in a town*.

2. It's *cold* / *hot*.

3. They're *helping* / *playing*.

4. They're going *by bike* / *on foot*.

B **Work in pairs.** Discuss.

1. How do you think the girls feel?

2. How do you help your friends at school?

A Listen and point. 🎧 TR: 7.1

clean up my bedroom

cook

feed the dog

fix my bike

go shopping

make my bed

practice the piano

take out the garbage

wash the dishes

water the plants

B Listen and repeat. 🎧 TR: 7.2

C Say.

How do you help out?

I cook breakfast and wash the dishes. How do you help out?

I take out the garbage.

A **Listen and read.** 🎧 TR: 7.3

We **never** sleep.	
We **sometimes** cook with them.	
He **usually** feeds the cat.	
My bedroom's **always** clean.	

B **Listen and chant.** 🎧 TR: 7.4

On Saturdays and Sundays
we help our mom and dad. Chores, chores.
We sometimes cook with them;
we usually feed the cat. Chores, chores.
My bedroom's always clean;
we practice the piano. Chores, chores.
We fix our bikes. We never sleep.
And then we play in the park!

C **Look and say.**

	Ivo	Anisa	Theo and Kati
go shopping			
feed the cat			
cook			
water the plants			

Ivo always goes shopping.

That's right!

Theo and Kati sometimes feed the cat.

No! They never feed the cat. My turn.

A girl watering the plants in her home garden

UNIT 7 **69**

A Listen and repeat. 🎧 TR: 7.5

plastic   leaders   planet   recycle

B Listen and read. 🎧 TR: 7.6

Children can help to make a difference in the world!

Melati and Isabel Wijsen are sisters from Bali, Indonesia. Bali is beautiful, but it has a problem. There are **plastic** bags everywhere—on beaches, in rivers, and in the streets.

The sisters go walking every day. They see plastic trash, and it makes them sad.

Melati and Isabel have a special group called *Bye Bye Plastic Bags*. The group helps **leaders** understand that plastic is bad for the **planet**. Now, people can't use plastic bags for shopping in Bali.

The sisters **recycle** old clothes to make new bags. They give their bags to stores in Bali. People can use the bags many times. Now, the plastic problem isn't as bad!

C **Read again.** Circle the correct word.

1. Melati and Isabel are **friends** / **sisters**.

2. Plastic bags **are** / **aren't** a problem in Bali.

3. The sisters go walking every **day** / **week**.

4. Now, people **can** / **can't** use plastic bags for shopping in Bali.

5. They make bags from **old** / **new** clothes.

6. They **give** / **sell** the bags to stores.

Melati and Isabel Wijsen, Bali, Indonesia

A **Listen and read.** 🎧 TR: 7.7

How often do the sisters go walking?

They pick up trash **every morning**.

People can use their bags **three or four times a day**.

The recycling truck comes **once a week**.

I feed the dog **twice a day**.

I help my mom **on weekends**.

B **Listen and underline the incorrect part.** Write the correct words. 🎧 TR: 7.8

1. On weekdays, Felix and Rita go shopping with their parents.

   _____

2. After Rita gets up each afternoon, she makes her bed.

   _____

3. Felix takes plastic bottles to the supermarket to recycle them twice a month.

   _____

4. Felix feeds the cat twice a day.

   _____

C **Look and say.**

clean up your room   help your teacher
ride your bike   wash your hair   watch a movie

You clean up your room twice a week.

No! I clean up my room every day.

You ride your bike on weekends.

That's right!

A **Listen and say.** 🎧 TR: 7.9

igh

nigh**t**

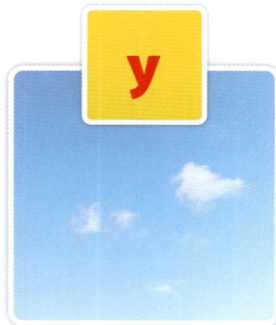
y

sky

i_e

ki**t**e

B **Listen.** Say the sounds. 🎧 TR: 7.10

n – igh – t	n**igh**t
r – igh – t	r**igh**t
m – y	m**y**
fl – y	fl**y**
r – ide	r**id**e
k – ite	k**it**e

C **Write** *igh*, *y*, **or** *i_e*. Listen and chant. 🎧 TR: 7.11

I feel all r____t
when I r____ my b____.
I sm____ every t____
I fl____ my k____.

D Write *igh*, *y*, or *i_e*. Say the words. Listen and repeat. 🎧 TR: 7.12

1.

crocod_____

2.

n_____t

3.

p_____apple

4.

Goodb_____e!

5.

r_____

6.

sk_____

E Play.

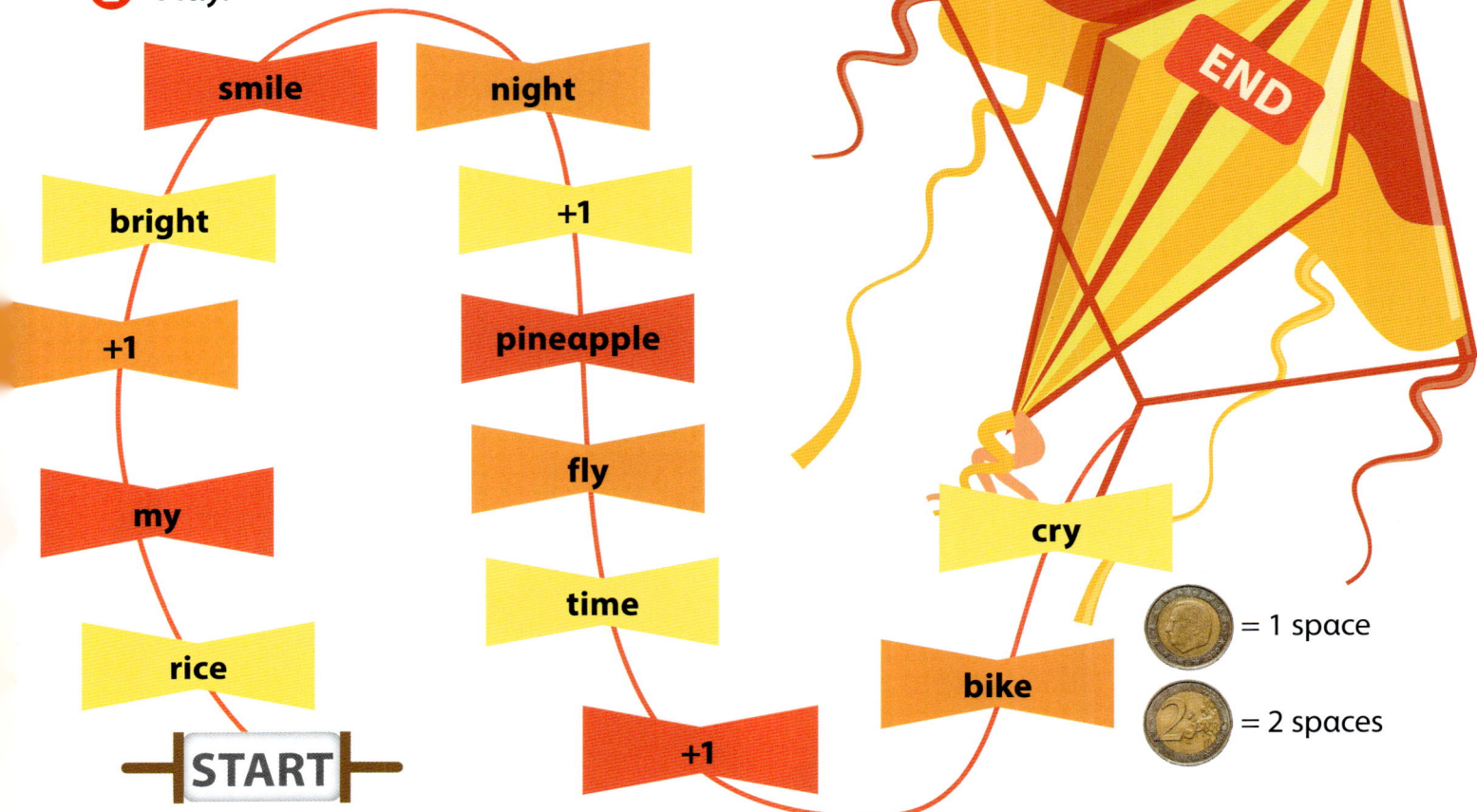

smile

night

bright

+1

+1

pineapple

my

fly

rice

time

cry

bike

+1

START

END

= 1 space

= 2 spaces

A **Listen, read, and write.** 🎧 TR: 7.13

I read my sister a story _____ night.
When it's broken, I fix my own bike.
I take out the _____ to help my family.
All week long, I try to do the right thing.

CHORUS

Do the right thing. It's the right thing to do.
Do the right thing. It's the right thing to do.

I _____ my bed every day.
I _____ the cat and make my lunch my own way.
I _____ up my bedroom. It makes me happy.
All week long, I try to do the right thing.

CHORUS

B **Listen and sing.** 🎧 TR: 7.14 and 7.15

C **Sing and act.** 🎧 TR: 7.16

A mother and daughter jump on a trampoline, Al Ula, Saudi Arabia

A **Look and circle.**

1. The girl is *jumping* / *swimming*.

2. The mother is *holding* / *getting* her daughter's hand.

3. It's *raining* / *sunny*.

B **Work in pairs.** Discuss.

1. Do you sometimes play like this?

2. What games do you play?

A Listen and point. 🎧 TR: 8.1

bake

collect stickers

do puzzles

dress up

make things

play hide-and-seek

play video games

read comic books

roller-skate

watch movies

B Listen and repeat. 🎧 TR: 8.2

C Say.

What hobbies do you have?

I bake cookies. What hobbies do you have?

I do puzzles.

A **Listen and read.** 🎧 TR: 8.3

> I **like** do**ing** puzzles.
> Jana **likes** play**ing** video games.
> Maz **doesn't like** read**ing** comic books.

B **Listen and chant.** 🎧 TR: 8.4

CHORUS
We don't like doing all the same things.
But that's OK! That's OK.

Maz likes doing puzzles,
but he doesn't like dressing up.
Jana likes dressing up,
but she doesn't like baking with her mom.
Me? I like baking with my mom,
and I like collecting stickers.
CHORUS

C **Find and say five things you and your friends like.**

I like roller-skating.

I do, too.

I don't.

I like playing hide-and-seek.

I do, too.

I do, too.

Yay! We all like playing hide-and-seek!

A Listen and repeat. 🎧 TR: 8.5

> stick   teenagers   interested in   real

B Listen and read. 🎧 TR: 8.6

> Hobby horses are toys for young children. A hobby horse is a horse's head on a **stick**. But now in Finland, older children and **teenagers** are still playing with hobby horses. They are doing it as a sport—hobbyhorsing. You run, dance, and jump, the same as you can do on a horse, but you do it with a toy horse!
>
> But do these children also like riding real horses? Yes, they do. Many of them are **interested in** horses. They practice so that they can jump very high and run fast, just like **real** horses! They practice walking like a horse. And if you like making things, you can make your own hobby horse.

C **Read again.** Write the correct word.

> jump   make   sport
> stick   teenagers

1. A hobby horse is a _____ with the head of a horse on the top.

2. Hobbyhorsing is a new _____.

3. It is very popular with _____ in Finland.

4. You have to _____ high to be good at hobbyhorsing.

5. Children can _____ their own hobby horses.

A Listen and read. 🎧 TR: 8.7

> Do the children like riding real horses?
>
> Yes, they do. / No, they don't.
>
> Does the girl like riding her hobby horse?
>
> Yes, she does. / No, she doesn't.

B Listen and complete. 🎧 TR: 8.8

1. _____ children _____ playing with hobby horses?

   _____, they _____. They are a popular toy.

2. _____ Alisa like _____ with her hobby horse?

   _____, she _____. She loves it!

3. _____ old people _____ hobbyhorsing?

   _____, they _____.

4. _____ your sister like _____ horses?

   _____, she _____. She thinks they're scary!

C Look and say.

	Riding horses	Playing soccer	Dressing up
Ed	✓	✗	✗
Sara	✓	✓	✗
Pedro	✗	✓	✗
Tina	✗	✓	✓
Jun	✓	✗	✗
Fatima & Neema	✓	✗	✓

> Does Ed like riding horses?

> Yes, he does. Does he like playing soccer?

> No, he doesn't.

A **Listen and say.** 🎧 TR: 8.9

ow

sn**ow**

oa

c**oa**t

o_e

st**o**n**e**

B **Listen.** Say the sounds. 🎧 TR: 8.10

w – i – n – d – ow   wind**ow**

kn – ow   kn**ow**

c – oa – t   c**oa**t

h – ome   h**o**m**e**

cl – ose – d   cl**o**s**e**d

C **Write** *ow*, *oa*, or *o_e*. Listen and chant. 🎧 TR: 8.11

Are you at h_____?
Can I call you on the ph_____?
I kn_____ it's sn_____ing,
but let's put on our c_____ts
and thr_____ sn_____ balls
at th_____ trees.

D Write *ow*, *oa*, or *o_e*. Say the words. Listen and repeat. 🎧 TR: 8.12

1.

yell_____

2.

rainb_____

3.

g_____t

4.

b_____t

5.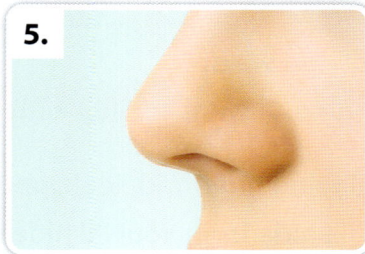

n_____

6.

h_____

E Spin. Say the word.

ow

oa

o_e

nose

stone

rainbow

road

home

snowball

show

coat

A Listen, read, and write. 🎧 TR: 8.13

Look out the window. It's _____! Oh, no!

We can't play soccer; we have to stay home.

The park is closed, so what can we do?

I _____ like watching TV. I want to play with you.

Do you like doing _____? No, I don't.

Do you like _____ cakes? No, I don't.

Look out the window. What can we do?

I don't like playing video games. I want to play with you.

I _____ playing hide-and-seek, and I know you like that, too.

Yes! You count to ten, and I'll hide from you! I'll hide from you!

B Listen and sing. 🎧 TR: 8.14 and 8.15

C Sing and act. 🎧 TR: 8.16

A Play.

Cable Cars!

END

14 How can you help your friends at school?

(page 67)

13 Write and say: I **always** sleep at n_____t.

(page 72)

12 Say three things you and your friends like.

(page 77)

8 She rides her bike _____ **weekends**.

(page 71)

9 Write and say the word: **yell**_____

(page 81)

10 Where do children do a sport with hobby horses?

(page 78)

11 Write and say: **never**, **sometimes**, _____, **always**.

(page 69)

7 Say the words: **coat**, **home**.

(page 80)

6 The recycling truck comes on Saturdays. It comes _____ **a week**.

(page 71)

5 I clean my room **every day**. My room is _____ clean.

(page 69)

4 Jana likes _____ **video games**.

(page 77)

START

1 Say two **chores** you do to help out.

(page 68)

2 Say two things you **like doing** after school.

(page 76)

3 Where are Melati and Isabel from?

(page 70)

Helping Hands

Christopher Nguyen lives in Alameda, California, US. He likes playing the piano. He is very good at it, too! He likes sharing his special talent. Every two weeks after school on Fridays, he visits the Waters Edge Lodge. It is a place for seniors. The seniors usually like doing puzzles and watching TV after dinner. When Christopher comes to play the piano for them, they all stop to listen.

Christopher likes making people happy. He looks at people's faces to see how they are feeling. Then he chooses the kind of music to play on the piano. He can play many different kinds of music. Usually the seniors smile, and sometimes they cry.

Christopher is usually very shy. He doesn't like talking in front of his classmates at school. When he plays the piano, he doesn't feel shy. He feels very happy. And he likes being with the people at the Waters Edge Lodge.

Glossary

talent something that you can do well

seniors people over 65 years old

cry what you do when you are sad

shy when you feel uncomfortable with other people

Christopher Nguyen at the Waters Edge Lodge, Alameda, US

A **Do you like music?** What kind of music do you like?

> I really like music. I like fast music because I like dancing!

B **Listen and read.** What does Christopher do every two weeks? 🎧 TR: 8.17

C **Read again.** Write the correct word.

> Fridays   happy   people
> shy   talent   talking

1. Christopher has a special
   _____ .

2. He visits the Waters Edge Lodge on
   _____ .

3. Christopher makes the seniors feel
   _____ .

4. At school, Christopher is usually very
   _____ .

5. He doesn't like _____ in front of his classmates.

6. He likes being with the _____ at the Waters Edge Lodge.

D **Say.** What do you like doing in your free time? How does it make you feel?

> I like dressing up.
> It makes me feel silly.

> I like playing video games.
> It makes me feel happy.

A Write the correct word.

> bed   bike   dinner   dog   piano   room   shopping   wash

On Saturday mornings, I make my _____ and clean up my _____.
I always remember to feed the _____. Then, I usually go _____ with my
dad. After lunch, my brother and I _____ the dishes. Then, I do my homework or I
practice the _____.

B Listen and match. 🎧 TR: 8.18

1. Emma likes _f_.
2. Fabio likes ___.
3. Fabio's dad likes ___.
4. Emma's mom likes ___.
5. Emma's brother likes ___.

a. baking
b. doing puzzles
c. making things

d. playing video games
e. reading comic books
f. roller-skating

C Write the correct words.

> every day   how often   on weekends   once a week   three times a week   twice a day

	Mon	Tue	Wed	Thurs	Fri	Sat	Sun	
1.	✓✓	✓✓	✓✓	✓✓	✓✓	✓✓	✓✓	I wash my face _____.
2.	✓		✓				✓	She rides her bike _____.
3.					✓	✓		We go to the park _____.
4.			✓					They have English class _____.
5.	✓	✓	✓	✓	✓	✓	✓	He sees his grandparents _____.
6.	?	?	?	?	?	?	?	_____ do you see your grandparents?

D Circle.

1. Do Ed and Lily like eating chocolate?

   a. Yes, they do.

   b. Yes, he does.

2. Do you like cleaning your bedroom?

   a. Yes, it does.

   b. No, I don't.

3. I like taking out the garbage.

   a. Do you? I don't!

   b. She does it.

4. My dad washes the dishes.

   a. Yes, he does.

   b. Does he like doing it?

Lesson 2   Present progressive questions and answers

Am	I			I	am.		I	'm not.
Are	you			you	are.		you	aren't.
Is	he she it	going?	Yes,	he she it	is.	No,	he she it	isn't.
Are	we they			we they	are.		we they	aren't.

Note: run + n + ing → running, sit + t + ing → sitting

Read and write.

1. Am I (play) _____ ?   Yes, you _____ .

2. _____ you sleeping?   No, we _____ .

3. Is he (eat) _____ ?   Yes, _____ .

4. _____ taking photos?   Yes, I _____ .

Lesson 4   Comparative adjectives: *-er than*

Use comparative adjectives to compare one thing with another thing.			
I'm	faster	than	my brother.
An elephant is	bigger		a rhino.

Note: big + g + er → bigger

Read and write.

1. Lions are fast. Cows are slow. → Lions are (fast) _____ .

2. A giraffe is big. A mouse is small. → A giraffe is (big) _____ .

3. This crocodile is small. That crocodile is big. → (small) _____

4. You're 8. Your brother is 12. → (young) _____

Lesson 2   *What's the weather like? It's + weather*

What's the weather like?	It's cold. / It's hot.
	It's cloudy. / It's sunny. / It's windy.
	It's raining. / It's snowing.

Note: cloud + y → cloudy, sun + n + y → sunny, rain + ing → raining

Look and write. Draw the weather in 4.

1. What's the weather like?
    _____

2. What's the weather like?
    _____

3. What's the weather like?
    _____

4. _____?
    It's raining.

Lesson 4   **Imperatives**

| Use the imperative to tell a person to do something. **Wear** your coat. **Put on** your boots. | **Note:** Don't = Do not |
| Use *don't* + verb to tell a person not to do something. **Don't wear** your scarf. **Don't bring** an umbrella. | |

Read and write. Use *Don't* if necessary.

1. It's raining. _____ your umbrella. (forget)

2. It's windy today. _____ your scarf. (put on)

3. You don't have gym today. _____ your gym shoes. (bring)

4. It's sunny today. _____ your sun hat. (wear)

Lesson 2   Questions with *How...?, When...?, Where...?*

How	do you get to school?	I go by bus.
When	does the bus come?	It comes at eight o'clock.
Where	does he eat lunch?	He eats lunch at school.

Read and circle. Then match.

1. How **do** / **does** they get to school?
2. When does the bus **come** / **comes**?
3. **When** / **Where** do you eat lunch?
4. **How** / **Where** does your mom get to work?

a. We eat lunch at school.

b. She goes by bus.

c. They go by bike.

d. It comes at eight o'clock.

Lesson 4   Plurals

	One	Two or more
+ es	beach	beaches
	box	boxes
	bus	buses
	dress	dresses
	fox	foxes
	mango	mangoes
	potato	potatoes
	tomato	tomatoes
No change	fish	fish
	sheep	sheep

	One	Two or more
y → ies	baby	babies
	family	families
	party	parties
f → ves	scarf	scarves
Other	child	children
	foot	feet
	man	men
	mouse	mice
	person	people
	woman	women

Write.

1. <u>tomatoes</u>

2. _____

3. _____

4. _____

5. _____

6. _____

Lesson 2   Simple past: *was, wasn't*

I He She It	was	good at school.
	wasn't	

Note: wasn't = was not

Read and circle.

1. Before, his face **is** / **was** dirty. Now, it **'s** / **was** clean.

2. When I **'m** / **was** little, I was loud. Now, I **'m** / **was** quiet.

3. The book **isn't** / **wasn't** scary; it was funny!

4. When my dad **is** / **was** little, he **is** / **was** silly and funny!

5. Before, I **'m not** / **wasn't** big. Now, I **'m** / **was** big.

Lesson 4   Simple past: *were, weren't*

You We They	were	famous.
	weren't	

Note: weren't = were not

Read and write.

1. My friends _____ (✓) naughty at school today.

2. We _____ (✗) silly at the park today.

3. You _____ (✓) cute when you were a baby.

4. We _____ (✗) very kind when we were younger.

5. They _____ (✗) quiet at the library this afternoon.

Lesson 2   Questions with *be*

	Questions	Answers
Yes/No questions	**Are** you **from** Brazil? **Is** she **from** Argentina? **Are** they **from** Japan?	No, I'**m not**. Yes, she **is**. No, they **aren't**.
Where...?	Where **are** you **from**? Where **is** he **from**?	I'**m from** Australia. He'**s from** the UK.

I'm = I am	we're = we are
you're = you are	they're = they are
he's = he is	isn't = is not
she's = she is	aren't = are not
it's = it is	

Write questions and answers.

1. __Where's he from__ ?   He's from Poland.

2. _____ Italy?   Yes, she is.

3. Are they from South Africa?   Yes, _____ .

4. Is he from Argentina?   No, _____ .

Lesson 4   Possessive adjectives

I	my	I have a new bike. **My** bike is pink.
you	your	Is **your** school nice? Are you happy there?
he	his	He plays badminton with **his** parents on Saturdays.
she	her	She read **her** story to the class. It was very good.
it	its	The soccer team has **its** own T-shirt.
we	our	We sometimes see **our** teacher at the store.
they	their	They bring **their** guitars to music class on Mondays.

Write *my, your, his, her, our,* or *their.*

1. This is Tomas. He's _____ big brother. People say I look like him.

2. She loves animals. _____ favorite animals are cats.

3. Petra and Giorgia have cameras. _____ cameras are new.

4. My sister and I often help _____ father at work. He works at a bookstore.

Lesson 2 Questions with *do/does*

Yes/No questions	Short answers	Affirmative sentences
Do you **live** in the US?	Yes, I **do**.	I **live** in Los Angeles.
Does she **live** with her parents?	No, she **doesn't**.	She **lives** with her grandparents.
Do they **live** far from here?	No, they **don't**.	They **live** on the next street.

Note: I/you/we/they **live**… BUT: He/She/It live**s**…
I/you/we/they **don't live**… He/She/It **doesn't** live…

Write questions with *live*. Write short answers.

1. Carlota / near her school? (✔)

   Does Carlota live near her school ? Yes, she does .

2. João and his brother / in an apartment? (✔)

   _____ ? _____ .

3. Lily's father / in the same town as Lily? (✗)

   _____ ? _____ .

Lesson 4 Prepositions of movement

Draw.

Use *above*, *across*, etc. to say where people and things are going.

	above		down
	across		past
	along		through
	around		under

1. A bird flies above a tree.

2. A boat goes under a waterfall.

3. A giraffe walks past some trees.

Lesson 2   Adverbs of frequency

Use adverbs of frequency to say how often we do things.

▮▮▮▮	always	▮▮▮	usually
▮▮	sometimes	▮▮	never

Note: Adverbs of frequency go before most verbs but after *to be*.
I **never go** to bed late.   She **is never** late.

Write. Put the words in the correct place.

1. Ali plays basketball. (sometimes)   Ali sometimes plays basketball._____

2. Samira and Adila go shopping on Sundays. (never)   _____

3. Haroun is in bed at nine o'clock. (usually)   _____

4. We watch TV at dinner time. (always)   _____

Lesson 4   *How often…?* and expressions of frequency

Asking questions		Saying how often			
How often	do you eat outside?	We eat outside	once twice three times	a day. a week. a year.
			every	day/week, etc.
			on weekends.	

Note: *once* = one time; *twice* = two times; *on weekends* = on Saturdays and Sundays

Write one word in each space.

Kenji and Haruto love sports. They play at school and _____ weekends. Kenji plays tennis once a _____ with Haruto on Tuesdays, but he also plays tennis with his dad _____ Sunday. Twice _____ month, he and his soccer team play against another team, but they also practice _____ a week – on Wednesdays and Fridays. Kenji doesn't like baseball, but Haruto loves it. He plays baseball three _____ a week.

Lesson 2 *Like + -ing*

After *like*, use *-ing* to talk about activities.

🙂	I **like** tak**ing** photos. She **likes** rid**ing** her bike.	🙁	I **don't like** mak**ing** my bed. He **doesn't like** wear**ing** socks.

Write what the children like or don't like doing.

1. Alice and Lily __like playing basketball__ . 2. We _____ .

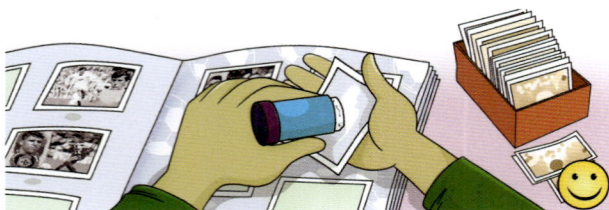

3. Ben _____ . 4. Olga _____ .

Lesson 4 **Questions with *like + -ing***

Yes/No questions	Short answers
Do you **like** cooking? **Does** she **like** playing with her little brother?	Yes, I **do**. / No, I **don't**. Yes, she **does**. / No, she **doesn't**.

Match and write the answers.

1. Does John like swimming?

2. Do you and Matt like watching movies?

3. Does Rachel like doing puzzles?

4. Do Keito and Miyu like flying kites?

5. Do you like riding horses?

a. No, I _____ .

b. No, she _____ .

c. Yes, he _____ .

d. Yes, they _____ .

e. Yes, we _____ .

Thank you to the educators who provided invaluable feedback during the development of *Imagine*:

EXPERT PANEL

Gracia Castillo, MOE - Basic Education
Maria Cristina Chiochetti Pinheiro, Colégio Pentágono
Andrew Duenas, ILA
Bouchra Elatraoui, Newton International School
Michele Gnan, Ningbo Concordia International School
Rina de Góngora, Colegio Jardín de las Rosas
Larisa Gribenkova

Aiko Hashimoto, Kyoshin Co., Ltd.
John Johnson, Language Link
Justina Kao, Ailin English School
Jye Liu, Zhuoyue Experimental School of Beijing Normal University
Tsutomu Mizutani, JO English School
Chi Hieu Nguyen, Innovative Education Group

Keiko Okazaki, Seikei Elementary School
Ghada Qaqish, Greek Orthodox School
Rachid Sif, Ecole Charles Péguy
Ana Carolina Torres Soares, Cultura for Schools
Andrew Whitmyre, Seikei Elementary School
Cindy Zhang, Dachang Happy School

REVIEWERS

LATAM

Gabriela Maria A. de S. Robaço, Wonder English
Valdomiro M. Arantes, AB
Laura Arizmendi, Colegio Bicultural San Patricio
Adriana Bermudez
Viviana Canulli, IEC Institute
Tatiana Chiquito Gómez, Universidad Pontificia Bolivariana
Leila Claro, Casa Branca Educação
Silvana Cristaldo, Britannia
Raquel Custodio, CSA
Erika Espino
Stela Foley
Sandra Milena Giraldo Valencia, Normal Superior
Estela Hermo, Instituto Friends English for Everyone
David Herrera, International Alliance of Academic Services
Cynthia Javes Rojas
Jussara Lazzarotti, Colegio Vimasa
Silvana Lemes, Colegio Parroquial San Carlos Borromeo
Martha Márquez, CENLEX Santo Tomás
Antonio Mendoza, I. Gestalt
Odalis Monzon Torres, IE Santa Teresita
Catalina Planes
Nélida Ramos
María Esther Ramos Uribe, Colegio Alfredo Nobel
Eugênio Rego, CCL Teresina
Anna Rehrig, Centro Cultural Paraguayo Americano
Alejandra Reyna Castro, UPES
Maria Salazar, Alborada
Carolina Sandoval, NSL
Sarah Schneider, EAFIT
Ayelén Schumich Ríos, Windlands Culturas y Lenguas
Miluska Tito Tejeda, Idiomas Universidad Católica
Ana Verde
Martha Verdesoto, Unidad Educativa Victoria Vasconez Cuvi
Lady Villanueva Cortez, Lidemperú
Marilia Zambolin S Goulart, Colegio Visconde de Porto Seguro

ASIA

Sameena Admani, Jubilee School
Stevany Melinda Anwar, Sekolah Kristen Pelita Kasih
Apple Jean Barcena, Don Galo Elementary School
Jingwei Cheng, Only International School
Lien Dang Hong, Che Lan Vien Upper secondary school
Hualin Deng, Shell English
Diana Dewi
Huong Doan, Kidtopi
Lucy Du, ABC
Le Du, Da Meng Shi Dai

Peter Du, JS International Learning Center
MC Go, English Center 英会話
Fuiyu Gotoh, Meet the World English School
Chloe Gu, QSH Primary School
Kishia Grace Hardiolen, Provincial Government of Palawan
Waly Horgeyor
Yuehang Hu, Easygoal
Yukako Kimura, St. Ursula
Ellie Kumagai, Ellie's English
Paramita Kusumawardhani, Sekolah Unggulan Indonesia
Mary Joyce Ladimo, Washington International School
Nga Le, Meta English Center
Florence Leung, Universal Education Center
Lis Lin
Amber Liu
Junko Matoba, KEC English School
Masako Miura, Hatchlink
Masumi Miyaki, English House Kobe
Dhanushka Kaushal Muthukudage, Royal Academy for Languages
Mari Nakamura, Mari's English Language Education Port
Sarah Nelson, ILA Vietnam
Nga Nguyen, TTCEDU
An D T Nguyen, Primary school
Van Nguyen, Kim Thach Primary School
Huong Nguyen, TDMU
Thảo Nguyễn, Gia Việt English Centre
Jeremy Ota, Berlitz Hamamatsu
Maricel Peralta, Deped
Imelda Prago, CNE1 International Language School
Idah Rahmah, Oak Tree Homey English Course
Abu Rahman, Crystal English
Janice Ralar
Cherry Reyes, Bethany Training and Consultancy LLC
Benhar Riman
Tiara Salam, Salam Homeschool
Coy Sarmiento, Alta Tiera Integrated School, Inc
Mia Serrano, University of Mindanao
Matthew Shapiro, Konan Boys' High School
Frances Shiobara, Kobe Shoin Women's University
Siswoyo Siswoyo, UMPRI
Paula Smith, Satoe Gakuen Elementary School
Wahyuningsih Soemiran, Ambassador School
Titut Sutyani, LIA
Mandukhai Suvd, Legacy Institute of Modern Education
Judith Tela, Ecology English Language Centre
Vu Thanh Trung, Kim Dong Primary School
Thinh Tran, Danang University
Quan Tran, Hoang Quan school

Thinh Tran, Danang University
Veronica Turnip, Penta Education
Elsie Vibora, Gifted Suksa Kindergarten
Roel Vicente, Tanchuling College Inc.
Sophon Von
Thu Vu, Cambridge Viet Foreign Language Center
Thanh Trung Vu, Kim Dong Primary School
Satoko Yamashita, ComEng English
Safriani Yusuf, SD YPS Singkole/Yayasan Pendidikan Sorowako
Jing Zhang, Uncle Sam
Magi Zhao, Plato Academy

EMEA

Shani Abell, Tuttolingue
Sori Ahmadi
Poppy Alexopoulou
Waleed Ali, Omar School
Marina Andrianopoulou, 4th Primary School Nea Ionia
Sohail Aslam, Govt. High School Kot Khaira
Syed Attia, Abdul Wali Khan University
Sefa Soner Bayraktar, Bahcesehir Koleji
Elena Belova
Ostap Bodyk, Mariupol State University
Natasha Borisavljevic, Piccadilly S Language School
Denisa Cani
Alisia Constantin, Miron Cristea Highschool
Rita Csontos, British International School Classic
Ana Cvijic, Big Ben
Andreea Ioana Daicu, Scoala Gimnaziala nr280
Loredana Dan
Mariam Darchia, MIA Academy
F. Beyza Dilbaz, Middle East Technical University
Dani Dimitrova
Luminiţa Melania Dîngă
Inna Dmytrenko, Boarding School 7
Jovana Drenjakovic, NSPRO Group
Zahra Ebrahimi, Emamat
Elena Efimova, Gymnasium # 652
Nataliia Filvarska, School № 33
Anil Gençer
Luminita Georgescu, Secondary School, Cornu
Tiziana Gilardi, I.C. Carducci-vochieri
Karolina Gołoś, Olympic Kids
Roxana I., Britanica Learning Centre
Nursima İKİZ, Gazi University
Gözde Katirci, KTU
Alona Khrupina, Eskişehir Bahçeşehir Koleji
Bela Koridze, School Olimpi
Tetiana Korotenko, lyceum 3
Maria Kouvarou, ABC
Raja Laribi, Mesaieed School for Girls
Eleonora Lazarova, Suiche "Sveti kliment Ohridski"
Aruba Malik, Pehchan

Polina Martinaitiene, Vydmantų gimnazium
Eva Mesogeiti
Brigitta Mod, Secondary School Mora Ferenc Zimandu Nou
Raluca Moldovan, Liceul Teoretic "George Moroianu"
Rehab Muhammad Mahmoud, MOE
Delia Nagy, Scoala Gimnaziala "Constantin Brancoveanu"
Rita Namajuškienė, Viekšniai Gymnasium
Marianna Nicoloyanni
Anna Nikolaeva, RCVR
Aslınur Okay, Turkish Ministry of National Education
Oksana Oliinyk, Brovary Educational Complex
Theodora Papapanagiotou, Papapanagiotou
Ludmila Pausova
Alisa Pejić, Osnovna Škola "Mejdan", Tuzla, BiH
Joanna Petrus, MOS 2
Maria Pinto, St. Julian's School
Liliana Pricop, Regina Maria
Fatima Rachbhare
Gabriela Rosca
Madalina Roscaneanu
Tetiana Ruda
Irina Rusina
Irina Šaripova, Klaipėdos Gabijos progimnazija
Georgianna Sarri
Pranvera Shehi, Mihal Ekonomi
Oksana Shtykh, School91
Khaled Siam, Taibah University
Alla Spizhova, Secondary school 108
Olga Starostina, School 15
Ecaterina Timofti, Theoretical Lyceum Natalia Gheorghiu
Marilena Ungureanu, "I.Al.Brătescu-Voineşti" School
Liudmyla Vakalo
Gitana Valkavičienė, Kaišiadorys Vaclovas Giržadas Progymnasium
Raluca Maria Voinescu, Gymnasium School Gura Ocnitei
Victoria Voudouraki
Karen Westra, Leeuwarderschoolvereniging
Rasa Zalnierukynaite, Ignalinos R.
Mohammed Zouli, M.E.N

US AND CANADA

Katherine Bailie
Erin Chang, MAP
Lourdes Ghazal, Ajial Bilingual School
Hope Newcomer, Catholic Charities Immigration and Refugee Services
Brian Ross, Oneida Herkimer Madison BOCES
Jennifer Strong, Little Star Learning Centre
Jeanine Wenzel, Community Action Inc of Central Texas

CREDITS